I've Got Dibs!

A donor sibling story

Story by
Amy Dorfman

Illustrated by
Darren Goldman

To Margaux
My Whole Heart
I Love You Most
And Then Some

XOXO
Mommy

One day I asked my mommy
about how I came to be.
She said "What a special
story" and explained
it all to me.

She picked me up and hugged me and
put me on her bed. She sat right down
beside me and this is what she said.

All my life I had a dream and my dream was to have you. But for me to have a baby I would need a man's help too.

I set out to find a donor.
A man who helps when you're in need.

What I asked for from this
donor was a special kind of seed.

for this seed is what I needed to help me
create you. But the best part is our
donor helped other mommies too.

Because of this kind deed many babies
would be made. For all these happy families
who had prayed and prayed and prayed.

All these kids
are called your
DIBLINGS
We call you
DIBS
for short. Your
DIBS
are like your
SIBLINGS
but a slightly
different sort!

You have the same
bright smile and that
twinkle in your eyes.
The fact that you're
related is really no
SURPRISE!

Your DIBIINGS share
your genes but not
the kind you wear.

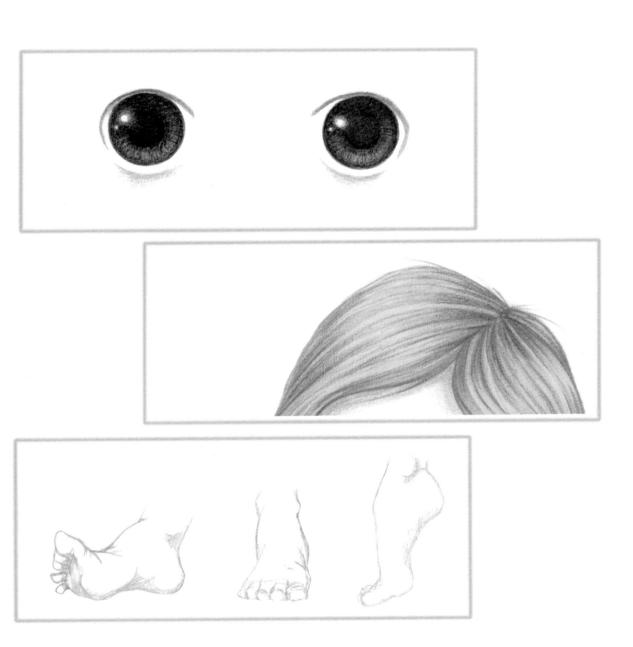

The kind that make you who you are:
Your EYES Your TOES Your HAIR.

Your DIBS are from all over.

All across the land.

There's enough of you to start
a DIBLING MARCHING BAND!

Or how about a SOCCER TEAM?

Perhaps a CHOIR too. Put you all together bet there's nothing you can't do.

The most important
thing though is the
bond that you all
share and knowing
if you need someone
there will be
somebody there.

My hope is that your DIBIINGS are something that you treasure. For this type of connection is something you can't measure.

When we started on this
journey I never thought
that we'd discover this
BEAUTIFUL EXTENDED FAMILY
that is truly like no other.

Now I know the story of how I came to be. Of all the special people who are a part of me. To keep it all together I just might need a chart.

Of all my awesome DIBLINGS who help to fill my heart!

MY DIBLINGS

NAME	STATE	COUNTRY

NAME	STATE	COUNTRY

A very special thank you to Isabella's friends. You are the icing on the cake. The cherry on top. Our very own "beautiful extended family that is truly like no other".

IXCMXCVI

Amy Dorfman (Author)

Amy is a single mother who started her family
with the help of a sperm donor. A year after her
daughter Margaux was born Amy read an article
about the Donor Sibling Registry, a database that helps
connect donor families. Within hours of registering Amy
was contacted by another family who used the same
donor. Six years and many connections later Amy and
Margaux are part of an extraodinary modern day family.
Amy hopes that by sharing this story, other families in the
same unique situation, will have a resource to share
with their children if and when they are ready to
connect with their own donor families.

Amy and Margaux live in the suburbs of Boston
with their two cats, Lucy & Ethel.
Amy has worked in marketing in the
retail music industry for over 20 years.
amydorfman@withanxpress.com

Darren Goldman (Illustrator)

Darren is a freelance illustrator living in Salem, MA.
A graduate of Columbus College Of Art and Design,
his work is often inspired by his love of animals and
growing up in the 80's. His work has been commissioned
by Newbury Comics, The Clarks Company,
Sire Records, Polaroid and Epson.

See more of his work at darrengoldman.com.

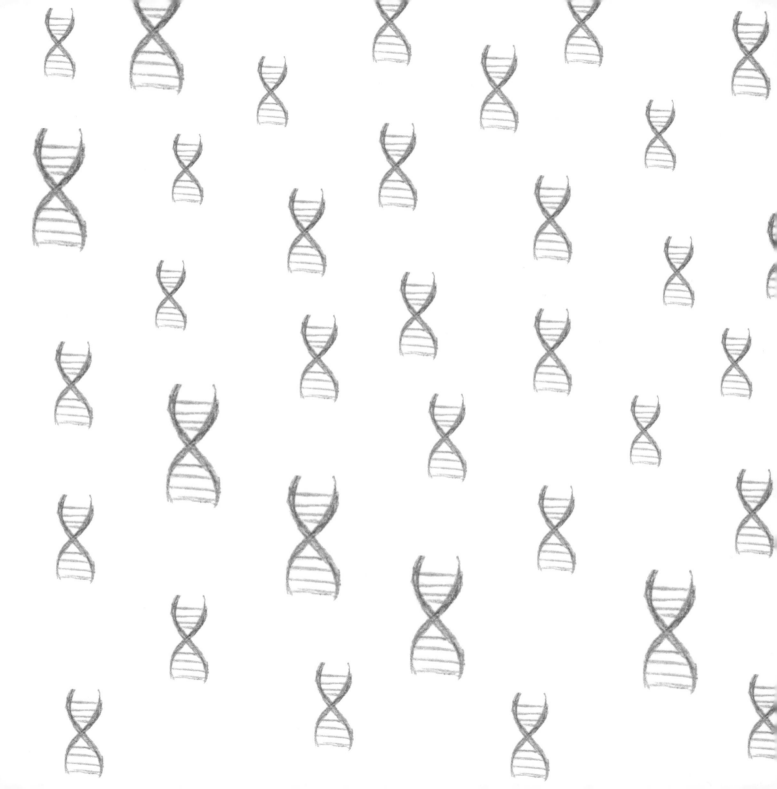

Made in the USA
Middletown, DE
22 August 2018